D0840625

SINA QUEYRAS

Coach House Books, Toronto

first edition, second printing

Published with the generous assistance of the Canada Council for the Arts and the Ontario Arts Council. Coach House Books also acknowledges the support of the Government of Canada through the Canada Book Fund and the Government of Ontario through the Ontario Book Publishing Tax Credit.

LIBRARY AND ARCHIVES CANADA CATALOGUING IN PUBLICATION

Queyras, Sina, author
    M x T / Sina Queyras.

Poems.
Issued in print and electronic formats.
ISBN 978-1-55245-290-5 (pbk.)

    I. Title. II. Title: M x T. III. Title: M times T.

PS8583.U3414M88 2014   c811'.6   C2013-907675-1

M x T is available as an ebook: ISBN 978 1 55245 375 9

Purchase of the print version of this book entitles you to a free digital copy. To claim your ebook of this title, please email sales@chbooks.com with proof of purchase or visit chbooks.com/digital. (Coach House Books reserves the right to terminate the free digital download offer at any time.)

I have my dead, and I have let them go,
and was amazed to see them so contented, so soon
at home in being dead...

                  – Rilke, 'Requiem for a Friend'

'Do not lecture me from sadness,'
lecture me from after, or under
sadness, from the scraping moment,
your forehead on coral, your feet
in the air.

                    – Anne Carson, *Grief Lessons*

ALTERNATING
MOURNING

With Alternating Mourning (AM), grief flows in both directions and may completely reverse itself. Far from being an unstable conduit for grief, AM allows for greater depth of feeling to flow more efficiently over greater distances. The downside to more deeply felt grief is a need for insulation to step down emotions for common transmission. Consumer mourning outlets vary according to countries, size of populations and equipment. The horizontal axis measures time, the vertical axis measures grief.

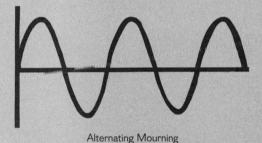

Alternating Mourning

Water, Water Everywhere

'I see' 'with my voice.' – Alice Notley, *The Descent of Alette*

Water, water, everywhere, my dead ones, and you wading through ferns to my window, a cat on a buoy, a rabbit on a paddle, a dog with a bowl in her mouth, water rising, water advancing and yes, yes, that is me, swimming through milk of sky, not a speck of barnacle underfoot.

Water, water, everywhere, bodies, gliding, feathered, furred, sweet pink and brown, your skins, you come to me with your blue eyes and your brown eyes, with your violet and green eyes, you come into my arms that hush and stride, Mother, Father, your legs that kick and strut, my pets, I carry you into my sleep, you come and I have saved my tuna water, I have made a meal of egg and rice for you, I have saved my best thoughts, too, I lay them at the foot of the bed and wait for you to slip under the door.

Water, my dead ones, and you with your ravaged look. It sometimes takes hours for you to face me, other times you have brought your own utensils, you come and I am open, you swim through my ribs.

My love, to love is to lose your love, to lose; the hand is emptied, if I turn away, if the rain stops, if I am silent … all the formulas for turning back time.

.

Grief is a century of death, and a century of death before that, and before that, I want to bring you into the fold, Death, I want to drag you right into the mall, the earth, which is made of death.

·

I think about Thích Nhất Hạnh smiling every time someone
puts her foot on the brake. I see the smiling Buddha in the brake
lights too, but more importantly I wonder how he drives in those
long robes and then I think of course he doesn't drive, and it's
easier to find the brake lights amusing.

I found the brake lights of the car I rear-ended last month alarming.
I was calling out to you, my dead ones, I was calling you home,
and I smashed into something solid and I forgot about breath.

·

I want to love my memory of you, it's not a conceptual feeling
though I can attempt a grid of my feelings for you, I can
calculate the number of verbs, and adverbs; I can leave a how-
to diagram on the coffee table if you would like to look at it
when I finally sleep.

·

I am feeling about you the way waves feel about the shore. You
come at me in endless loops, your moods, the looks on your
faces, my lost ones, more alive by the minute, and the colour in
your faces tinting with the seasons.

·

I am not interested in what Bourdieu, or Kristeva, has to say
about grief. I don't want a grid, I want arms. I don't want a
theory; I want the poem inside me. I want the poem to unfurl
like a thousand monks chanting inside me. I want the poem to
skewer me, to catapult me into the clouds. I want to sink into
the rhythm of your weeping, I want to say, *My grief is turning
and I have no way to remain still.*

I am not interested in feeling by proxy; I go to the hollow when I want to empty, I go to theory when I want to sit with someone else's thinking, I go to myself when I want to see you.

.

I am feeling about clover, I inhale and it honeys my lungs: if I finally do catch you and put my mouth to yours you will taste that summer.

When I am being torn apart, I don't need you to point out the empty seed pods of winter.

You won't find a couplet in the wild, my love; a sestina is a formal garden, a villanelle is the court, a sonnet is an urban love story, an epic is the senate, a prose poem is the city.

.

I am not interested in other words for honey. I am interested in honey.

.

I saw Mary Oliver on Cypress. The rough angles of the coastal mountains terrified her. Later she appeared on Spanish Banks looking west. *Distance is helpful*, she said, *but size isn't: this is too raw for poetry.* I dropped her in Stanley Park, I thought she might be more comfortable wandering the groomed paths.

.

I am operating on instinct here, the way the guy at the beach chooses his rocks to stack and the rocks never topple, they are grey on grey against grey, modular bodies, sturdy, flat, fat as islands.

I can't be worried about offending Mary. I can't weigh my grief against a pound of flesh. I have a right to order the driftwood or not. Whole nations have been built on description.

.

Mourning, like a thigh appearing in the blue light of winter.

.

Choose your memories well, my love, death is a long meditation.

.

Wanting is exhausting; in death have we let yearning go?

.

I read Mary Oliver's poem about angels dancing on the tip of a pin and I kept thinking, *She is writing about a penis, Mary Oliver is really a gay man and everything is about* AIDS, which made me want to carry Mary Oliver in my pocket.

.

How many shapes will you visit me in, Death? How many gestures – each a stitch in the belly. The entire woodland echoes with your filthy mouth, the neon tree, the leaf flickering a sequin in green velour, my flickering rock, my soft bowl, my leafy gasket, you bring me thoughts of the purest vials of amphetamine. You burn like the skin of a spider, laugh with the bounce of a rabbit, and yes, I do remember Spanish Banks, the city a diorama in Le Creuset, and later, burning your prescriptions in a cucumber mist, that heron appearing suddenly, so casual in his faded Chelsea coat, his prehistoric beak and yellow eye watching as I burned enough OxyContin to tile a small bathroom.

.

Sappho says in the house of song there shall be no mourning, but all song is mourning. All shapes reflect absence; I have collected all the bits of soap, every trace that can still float, and strung them from the rafters.

I am here with my flesh and my thoughts, trying to let go of you.

.

I see you in the Carolee Schneemann, banging the floor with a broom. I see you in the black, stacked shapes of Louise Nevelson, I see you in Andrea Zittel's *Escape Vehicle*, we are floating from island to island. I see you in Metro Pictures, there are endless reels of you moving stones from one side of a field to another. Who would you have been had you understood realism? Blood pooling in fur cups, boardrooms filled with hundreds of babies? A screen the shape of a jellyfish floating through a park? You can give a girl a cleaver but you can't make her swing.

Under all that rage, joy, big as the pills in Damien Hirst's mirrored cabinet, a caplet so huge you could parasail across the bay.

.

Good attracts good and so on.

The emergency of women is the emergency of the world. We say, *What good is history if we have not felt it?* We say, *Don't let the dead go until you have tasted them.*

.

How does one see? A thing in movement, a pail attached to a tall spiky wood, snow, spring, light? What is the beetle carrying? How banana a slug? What temperature mist? How glisten the leaf tremble?

Judith Butler at Princeton on the ethics of violence. The 'I' cannot tell the story of how it came to be – we may only become self-knowing by engaging in non-judgment. The self that propels the narrative is no longer, but the narrative goes on.

Who is that narrative?

Who is I?

Who is happy?

Who is singing? Who are we singing to? Ruth? Shulamith? Solomon? Son of Samuel? Buddha? Mother? Is it the man with no hands on the subway floor? Is it the last iceberg? Is it Dada? Is it you, my love?

.

Fuck you, you say, *fuck art, fuck cancer, fuck your empty gestures, fuck every way we are contained, every way we are numbed, fuck your female heroes with their trembling lips and short tethers.*

Fuck the way you see me as a fence post, fuck fence posts. Fuck the way you rely on women's work. Fuck the way you absent us from your conversations. Fuck Bellow, fuck Olson, fuck Berryman, fuck rhetoric, fuck you.

Take this anger; wipe your face with it, take your career and douse it in kerosene, walk away from it, you do not do, you do *not* do, grief, in your pointed shoes.

Everything has been critiqued, everything has been photographed, Diane Arbus took advantage of the freaks, Lee Miller finally turned the tables on the gaze, but she photographed more death than she made surreal masterpieces.

My love for you floats across architecture, lets the wind lift its skirt, refuses to be tamped down.

I am not angry – what smart person wouldn't want to fuck art? Or fuck in art? Or be fucked by art, her clean lines so hard and bright?

I call you from Matthew Marks, from Gagosian, tracing the lines of a huge Richard Serra curve. I have seen so much thinking gleaming, I want to roll it too, make it big, manly, I want to ride it through Manhattan, but mostly I want it solid, a deep root tethering me, an unflappable sense of calm. Are you calm now? I see you in the Arbus retrospective, furtive glances at the journals, you want to be angry but you can't stop looking and when you look you love and when you love the entire world unfolds around you, you are so bright you make the security guards flinch, lurch, pat the mics on their chests.

.

The future at a hundred miles an hour, mouths stretched like windsocks. I hate your seamless layers, you know that, but you scratch by, and I am thinking of all the Trojan horses this bay has seen, eleven of them now, bobbing in the harbour, containing who knows what army of product.

Unbelievable views, never did take them for granted. There is a spot just outside the pillar and glass where, when you stand in the pea gravel and whisper to me, standing where I am standing by the totem at the edge of the continent, we can hear all the dead ones singing.

DIRECT
MOURNING

Direct Mourning is the gold standard of consumer grief. The first line above measures time, the second line measures current. With direct mourning there are no surges of feeling, no outbursts; it is unidirectional, a consistent, even, unconscious current.

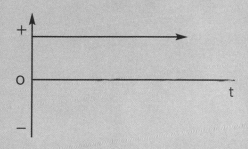

Current (F)   The quantity of emotions passing a given point
               (unit: feeling)

Voltage (M)   Pressure or force of grief (unit: memory)

Resistance (S)   Resistance to the flow of mourning (unit: sentiment)

Power (G)   The work performed by emotion (unit: grief)

Potential difference   The difference in voltage between the two ends of a
                        body through which emotions flow. Also known as a
                        memory surge.

*D*ear One, the future has crumbling infrastructure and more rain than ice, but there we are, peeking out like the tiny flowers that appear in the cracks under sills. Dear One, I am struggling to be in my body, struggling to stay where I am; I want to be closer to my memory of you. I am adrift without it.

Here in this city that does not love me, the sky falls like sheets of concrete, my days are a loud vertical assembly line of grey, crowding out the loops of pinks and purples, but no longer joy. The gentle men of my gym line up at the window on Papineau, shins in hand, heads turned momentarily away from the hockey game to the trees still trembling from autumn's threading.

Dear One, I can't shake you. It's my fault I am unhappy here. I am the only tree on the block refusing to let my leaves fall. I ride the light; I ride the future thinking of crinoline and cold white wine.

A Manual for Remembering

I wear [your] boots all summer long …
      — Stevie Nicks, 'Nightbird'

When remembering it is best to wear pants without cuffs, boots, gloves, safety glasses and a feeling helmet (shade 10 or higher).

·

I worry about open spaces. Wetness. But I also worry about walls, about feeling in confined spaces. I worry about the lilies. Do they have sufficient insulation? Is there an electrode holder under the furrow of beans? Will the earth hold my idea of it? Will it hold my idea of me? Is all this thinking sustainable?

He says the lilies are thrilled with the roots of poems, as if the lilies have stepped up and whispered this in his ear. He says the frogs know how the poets lie about nature. If the area is well lit you can plug in. He says when feeling it is best to have good insulation.

·

All mature poets understand the need for dry wood chips.

·

She understands the interrogative to be male. Instruction is also male. Certain forms of syntax elude her. If you can't speak with authority please remain silent. Always recharge your batteries before you attempt to cross topics. Hesitation is abject. Women rarely pull off certainty in public.

·

Are you are you not natural? Do you nurture? Do you recombine flora and fauna with electronics and machine parts? Can you accurately describe the experience of rainfall? Crowd grieving? Do you wear wool socks? Do you have a slot for cold-weather texting?

Never touch a banana slug, or cedar melting like lava. Beware of a failed city tumbling into the bowl of an upturned tree. If ferns adorning each dull ache are wet, apply a Cowichan sweater zipped up to the first branch.

.

It may well be the same day: we warned you about touching the faces. If you know the feel of pavement, the sound of the shopping cart careening toward a not-yet-developed patch of forest, you should move to higher ground. If you have no control over your memories and they are of a constant voltage, minimize exposure to skin, use a semi-automatic memory welder with an excessive emotion-reducing device.

Keep all memory-carrying devices in good repair. Do not engage with damaged vessels. If insulation is missing do not use. If the seal is broken discard immediately.

Keep the memory zone clear, comfortable. Allow your thinking to thin out along the soup spoon of side roads; those roads with their litter of shoes will soak up the worst of it. If you hear her best intentions clamouring inside your head, or if there are sudden rhymes:

> knock, knock, who's there
> an atom
> an atom who?
> anatomy
> of a past not let go …

Galvanize yourself, stay on course.

·

I see people, she said,
some so sad they hurl themselves
off bridges,
into traffic, out of moving vehicles,
or more positively, so full of joy they hurl themselves
into the bruise of morning
wanting to have known more,
wanting to have loved more,
and not afraid to bleed, they open
hearts like umbrellas
and leap.

·

Be wary of the position of your head. A lack of ventilation is dangerous. Minimize exposure to heavy, or random, emotions. Read warnings. Consult safety data. If you cannot leave the area, use special care when remembering past lovers. Perspective, perspective. If you can't be positive, at least be consistent!

Don't paint yourself into a corner. Ask yourself, *What would Diane Arbus do?*

·

She says rogue memory rays can cause a burning sensation. Select a filter before approaching the past.

Always use a tether when feeling in public. Never dive in alone.

Wear clothing that protects the skin. Avoid cathode rays. Keep bodily functions, organs, neatly organized.

Remember, clutter kills: there is no reason for the past to be disorganized.

.

She draped her memories over the spine of Virgil,
she lounged into Sappho,
they slept in the pause between verses, fingers
touching the pink afterthought
of sex.
I would recognize that peony anywhere, he said,
his cheeks bristling with her, his tongue
in the gutter of her page.
Peony, she repeated, but even then she was thinking carnation.
Poppy Authority is not so much loud as insistent.

.

Diane Arbus never experienced adversity in her childhood. She had adequate ventilation. She had a small lens in her head just above the brow.

.

When in doubt, wear lipstick. Also, carefully evaluate ventilation, cables, connectors. Work as closely as possible to the area where remembering is being performed. Apply shades evenly, keep a fresh tube of Chanel on hand.

Use only double-insulated gloves. Steel-toed boots. Be sure all ideas are grounded, all equipment disconnected before service. If using auxiliary power be sure to use skin protection of spf 90 or higher. Do not remember in a windstorm, or heavy rains.

For chance encounters, touch the back of her knee.

Never touch the knee with an electrode. Never lift a memory with a body attached. Lightly apply scent before leaving the house, understand that the past is an aphrodisiac: always keep it upright, out of inclement weather, away from all explosives or corrosives, chained to a firm support.

.

The moon is tossing money:
the path is lit by knots of
you, the many and the one you,
eyes so hungry they will gnaw
through tar. There are many places
she wants to burrow her head.
Remembering you is one of them.

CIRCUIT
SYMBOLS

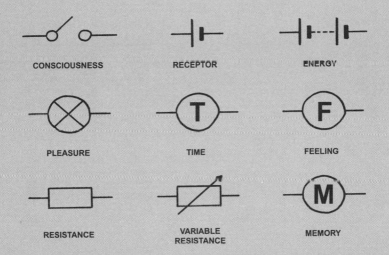

CONSCIOUSNESS   RECEPTOR   ENERGY

PLEASURE   TIME   FEELING

RESISTANCE   VARIABLE
RESISTANCE   MEMORY

On a lighter note, Dear One, sometimes while standing at my cutting board I think, What if women really are androids?

How good we have become at hashtags, and how distanced from our bodies, I walk in mine so surprised to feel anything. Such sustenance does not come from good woman apples.

Today I give in and buy the Oil of Olay anti-aging cream because though I like wrinkles, I might like them soft. I still want a face, Dear One, I want a body, I still want to be a light in the world.

The earth under cedars along the seawall makes my skin soften too; I spend hours each day with my memory of you, sensing time reverse. Is there a cream made of that? The-fir-in-sky-cedar-bed-children-with-pompom-hats-and-gulls-crashing-under-a-red-balloon cream?

An Irish legend concerning hairless men came to me and, stupidly, I opened it thinking, you know, how much Irish improves a poet. Meanwhile the sun ekes out every bit of joy from the cat, her tongue raking like an old Gaelic wheel.

Such lovely company your memory is, and on the train today a sweet man from Turkey upright as a maypole.

Like a Jet

Little streams passed all over their bodies.
      – Walt Whitman, *Leaves of Grass*

1

A hole in the sky where softness hung,
A crater where the world was, a moment
The size of Manhattan: amazed
We are not all sliding in.

I skirt abjection, drag my nails against
The hours. My eyes for one more glimpse,
Ochre (August, the rough tear of cotton,
The lace and wire, a harness of

Clinging). There is no shrugging off
Weight, no exit ramp, no ease or release,
Perpetual shoulders on orange alert, jaw
Scraping the floor, the body contorts,

The body is fluid: I am leaking,
I no longer care who sees me leak.

2

I held her briefly at the end because finally
She could not scowl me away. Felt her unlatch,
A small mass, rocketing like helium, body
Already a swelling replicate of self.

I could see no verve, no afterburn, no spirit
Lingering, just my empty reaching out:
How the dead can cower on the wing of
A plane or, like a missile, shoot out of sight.

Muffled drum of heart, my lungs, aging boxers
Swelling in a crow storm, hungry as Buck
Mulligan for her words, I chew them now,
Hollow seed pods catching on my tongue,

Those whiskers of good intention: sad
Eliot's jet, as if hoarding, gorging, on pain.

3

Every last vein crammed with absence. Hers
Yours, ours, I must return to the now. Two
Incompatible screens, the pixelated grief,
The polyurethane grief, stuffed, animated,

Shrunken sweaters aping across an abandoned
Gym, Sexton's arms outstretched, smoky
Scotch a glass clinking across the honeyed floor.
I await your return and, with it, futures

Uncorking. Hold tight, spray of time, we don't
Race to death, it comes at us; there is no safety fence.
Once you drop, you walk into the forest as though
You owned it, you turn, wave, inhale black of day,

Exhale sight. Inhale death, exhale life, Ozymandias:
Everything that lives is light and she is now dark.

4

Time, they say, time, and with it healing but also
Recrimination and upset, my tumourette an airbag
Behind my eyes, blind me, my lack of patience:
Why is my exuberance rewarded? Hers snuffed?

Siblings crumble slow, unremarkable
As fences across the prairie. Who set the bar
So low? Who has tagged her foot? Mine?
Those red lines traced across a chest,

A lung split open: hard pebbles of light
Pelt your ease. Those high-wire walkers vibrating
In the pain know something of loss's
Hammer, a persistent drum kit open under

The eave where pincers crack
A fly skull.

5

She is everywhere, the widening screen,
A surge in the weather, pages blooming,
Lines with animal movements, useless stalking.
I stare into the soup, trying to ignite some memory

Of eating. Sweet rain where Raven, carrying summer
Storms, stomps the air: a bull, head ready to draw
The sky closed. The more death we know the closer
We are, and yes, the onward path, packed with guilt

And smart knots where pleasures show. I go to
August with her horses, to the clover path under
The power lines. There is no traceable reaction to
The arbutus's shedding while all else blooms, we

Upswing and trill, tunnel our emotions. No more death
Please: bite hard, I want to feel the future coming.

6

I felt something snap just now. It wasn't you parting
Your body – it's months after that, as if all this time
Grief has been spinning our heels and now we slow, steady,
Let it nestle into a fold with the lost coins and lint.

Where you were, the sawed-off limbs of a birch, a scorch
Of concrete, a hemline, shoulders wedged, socks like muffins
Oozing out of jeans, fashion is also exhausted, and who
Cares about whims, please save me from abstraction.

Who will sort the apples? Leonard. Leonard will sort the
Apples. Frederick will drive the car. Jack will feel for you.
Describing is owning. Give me a woman with a lens
In her hand. Give me a woman with a will to read.

Give a woman a lost woman, an open vista, a stack of vellum,
Give me Time, give me swagger, give me your ears.

7

All the gods know is destinations. I have raised
A glass, my eye, your hook. Let's face it, the world
Is a shrinking place and hungry: too much grief
To feed. I float away from you on hard

Covers. I step out on the stacked hours. Words
If they were soil, I would throw them back into the
Compost pile and wait for spring. Those 'this is how
It is' speeches appear and later diamonds soft as bullets.

I went to the library looking to scaffold my thoughts.
Sure, now you say Lucretius. Intelligence is so often
Hindsight. Outside Holly Golightly's townhouse
There are taxis. The end of me, or you, is of no concern.

Frederick Seidel anoints me with the head of his penis.
It is soft as a chamois and spreads like egg across my scalp.

EMOTIONAL OVERLOAD
SENSOR CIRCUIT

The best way to measure emotions in a circuit is to place an emotion buffer in the current path. The higher the resistance, the more exact the measurement will be. However, the drawback of a high resistance is that it affects the operation of the circuit in which the measurement is being made. If an active buffer is used, the sense resistance can be kept small. The circuit diagram shows how an emotional overload indicator can be built using an emotion buffer and memory detector in the current path.

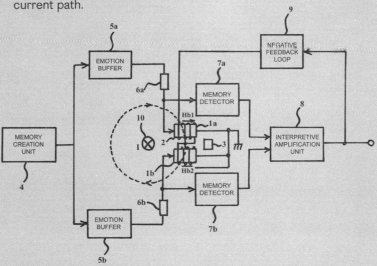

*T*here you are, Dear One, coiled in a garden, a hiss in the squelch of past where earlier I cut the eyes of seed potatoes and planted them two lengths deep. The sky, wet wool, weighed the garden and me, feet like trowels parting the past, chickens behind me gorging on worms, Mary's deer beyond the hash stump, a trio of tulip eaters nuzzling.

I have no deer, no stumps, no potato patch on the Plateau. It is not eat or be eaten; here my body moves through time. That was a pre-screen moment. That was paradise without LED or LCD or Thunderbolt Display.

Which is to say, we walked into it. So clean: the wind has licked the marrow from your bones and my fingerprints from mine, the forest has been subdivided, the deer stand ornamental, not daring to shit.

.

It's true, the roots of trees travel like neurons, carry sparks of fire for miles underground, and here we live on a cyborgian island, tear away and expose the runnel of wire and track and rats. It's true, at this distance, the hairs on your forearm fire like tiny strikes of lightning, and here the roads open up and swallow city buses whole.

.

We imagine Eliot's mind alone in the hollow, how men move like architecture into the landscape and take stock.

Of the Hollow

We've come here to hide. We aren't sure how we measure up. We are all craft. We bury our hearts and embrace the chore. We leave our thoughts in the trunk. We are suspicious of feelings. We doubt sentiment. We are tired of confession but feel silenced. We need to speak. We fear the all heart and no craft. We dread the all craft and no heart. We circle outside of ourselves wanting in, we circle inside of ourselves wanting out; we walk with the wall of the world in the dead centre of our gaze and we can never see beyond it.

We are terrified of our talent, of the cost. We cower in the clearing. We shrink in the salal. We have come to the sanctum, the green, with our desire to be washed clean. We stand on the threshold of our own creation and spit. We think, *If we could only walk with a spindle on our forehead, if we had a horse we could fill with all of our loves, if we could enter the vaulted city with our families in tow.* Instead we turn to the forest. We peer into the spores. We have our knees locked. How will we be women without using the birth canal? We want to cut off our bottoms, we want to be rigid, unyielding. We lie in the clearing and let the rain come. We lie with our feet touching. We lie with our faces open. We want to be strong. We think of the women.

Anne Cameron has a face carved out of cedar.

Daphne Marlatt with her words a peak of foam.

Helen Potrebenko driving a taxi across the bay.

There is a war canoe made of conceptual poems. It floats with a small town of angry women, a ghost warrior in a grass cape takes up the rear, the canoe floats high on the inside passage and knows no one's name.

On the islands, beyond the fringe, we circle our stumps and dream of casting off. We walk side by side with our cameras strapped, we see everything in twos. With our feet in step. With our hips in check. We walk in plaid with our jeans rolled up. We walk wet with seaweed in our ears. We turn the key. We pump the gas. The rain is falling and we want to move. Dark figures approach us, one rain-slickered arm up like an awning. We will take our punishment. We will roll over and cry.

We dread the quaint, the tubed lawn furniture. We dread the empty knots of language. We twist them, stack them, we want them for kindling. We dread the time bombs, inevitable, random.

We sleep back to back. We peer into the cavern. We rock on our heels, our feet squelching in nostalgia. We are fools. We think we know love. We think we have moved ourselves. We extend our arms like branches through grapes, we stare into the serrated night. We think our beginning is the beginning. We turn the clock back. We turn our faces back. We turn our backs. We load the stove with wood. We listen to it burn. The rain, the stove, we are hot. We turn and face. We turn and face. We are not in Manhattan, we have not understood how to frame what we see. We peer up at the wet mountains, we peer down at the sea; we are vertical with our desire.

We want to cradle the slopes.
We say Cypress is our child.
We say Grouse too.

We say the ocean is our lungs, we move through it daily.

We say the blackberry bushes are poking through our ribs.

We say our bodies frame everything if you can turn and look, our hands, burrowing into the brambles laid like thick bales of barbed wire.

We want to thumb through nature, we want it beautiful, ordered, containable. We want it to remain and yet we want to enter it like a gallery, cool, smooth, minimal, ordered in leather, elegant as Le Corbusier. We want to dwell in Charlotte Perriand, we say Arthur Erickson has not slept in a slit. We say we want colour. We want the new pristine. We want the reclaimed wild. We want California Closets. We want to file everything in small display cases. In drawers. Gold-embossed moss, pewter cases filled with bits of leaf fragment. Pouches of dried marigold. Pouches of iris. Pouches of wax. We love our pouches. We love our order. We want more pouches inside our pouches. We are encased even as we move through the air. We move and compile. We are an economy of women grieving.

We want to know how to be women artists in the world. We want to know beyond recipes for jam, beyond the thick brush strokes of pre-modernist canvases, we want fleeting and concrete. How to enter the mind of the world? How be a megaphone? How not to think in code? Thinking in public terrifies us. We hide, so tentative we think the wind might break our bones and yet we come to the clearing, we cannot contain our thoughts.

We come smelling of tadpoles and silt. We come mossy and sprouting feathers. We come in our layers of fleece, with pain in our groins. We come with our skins like sheaves of dew. We come, we are all of our shortcomings, we come through love like militiamen elbowing through razor wire. We come, rolling up our flaws, ready to dig in. We come wrapped like maypoles. We come in leather and lashed sprigs of heather. We are all of our flaws. We are ragged with imperfection. We bash ourselves against lithe hips. We aim, we fall short. We limp into the amber moments, sheepish. We are bent with emotion. We are uneven in our ability to move forward, we say, *Beware of the empty boat,* but we are often, ourselves, the empty boat.

·

The sum of its parts is not rose, not fern, not lichen, not spore, not granule. Several trees gave way to breeze. I dreamed I was liquid. The air like foil soothed me, the hours turning on the wings of Raven. I want a camera so small I can strap it like tefillin to the forehead of a bird and soar. Naturally this happens.

·

I want to say the sun never rose before this moment.

The past is always scantily clad.

EMOTIONAL
FIELD

Although emotional and nostalgic fields were experienced much earlier, the study of emotional fields as discrete objects began in 1269 when French scholar Petrus Peregrinus de Maricourt mapped out an emotional field on the surface of a spherical magnet using sharp memories

*D*ear One, better to patter, better to punt, better to butter my nest,
my bird dog, better end my nub, my inside weather, my nettle of
phrases, my stockpile of verbs, my heirloom nouns, lime of image, tick
of cedar, my sepia wood, pea gravel, concrete totems, tock of glass;
come low, Dear One, come near, come one, come push, slow push,
push back doubt, ward off stasis, heart rain, heart rain, porous
weather with her huge leaves, with her long waves, with her floating
cities and highways, her folding gridlock, her downy limbs, high, high
as seabirds eyeing herring from the clouds.

.

Doubt my rain, my love, eat my fear, my inside ferns, my nub of cock,
my root lungs, my green callus, my water columns, my sea cucumber,
my urchin, my Valiant green, cower in capes, my owlet, my cowl neck,
my outlet, my lining in hooks, my hooked metaphors, come lichen,
come moss, come caper, come cougar with your soft portals, come doe
with your thin springs, come childhoods with your fist of leashes,
come, my modernist loves, and latch a past in a Jell-O mould, float
my heart in a rose bowl, my sincerity in a flan, I would be ornamental
for you, I would spread, I would, like the hook of barbed wire, my
other half useless without the knot, and coil my lamp for you.

Five Postcards from Jericho

Dear Regret, my leaning this morning, my leather foot, want of stone, age old, my burnished and bruised, hair lingering, hand caked, spongy as November, my dear Relentless, my dear Aging, your voice tinny, dissonant as Stein shot through decades of war and Fortrel, cocktails on the hour, Zeppelins over Piccadilly, bombing blindly in the fog. Dear Skin, dear tobacco mouth. My refusal, my merely geographic, my fibrous strings for you: your abundant wit, your lack of shadow and still *joy, joy, joy*, nosing the air. Each moment stretches toward you, your dry feet: I carried them, pumiced and peppery, laid them where regret is a biscuit thing to lean upon and sweeten, my hour of you, my cursive thoughts, a pulpit beating under these ribs.

Dear Time, you swallowed us whole, swallowed us lovely, sharp as bones crimping underfoot, my benign, my flotsam and crabs thin as leaves, your smoothing, your sinking in. Mornings or mooring, or wallowing Jericho: tapioca air indolent. I am still there, supple and driftwood, you lovely, you loved me, your memory dark and west, thoughts like tugboats stitching the horizon, you pulling me, my pudding, my thin crustacean, my biscuit, sideways in the late afternoon, your gaze, having so soon forgotten the sharpness of mornings, the bite of your look serrating the hour: my treasures, all of them, for the pleasure of that slice once more, of our dangling, you and me, the lot of us in some car, driving some hour, mapless.

Under a spiderweb, a tire, slouched: flat, sad-lipped, I think of Newton, of the original apple, of all these clones since, all these scentless descents. I shake my glass, shake again, melted suffixes tinkling; observe all things natural: foliage unfurling like old bills, wryly betraying your habits, like the dog who digs and rubs, the dog who whines, who paws and circles. Why is pain so much better than nothing? Or the mark of it more recognizable? Why is saying nothing so much better than airing? Your one-liners like blossoms, uplifting, your currents strap me to air, yes I guess there is a little texture up here, and oxygen pure as baby's toes, which, if I recall, are sweet as kernels of corn, if I recall so long ago.

To arrive is practice, conversation or conversion, a story over a field, my sweet, of concrete or whispering, furrows of a path no longer, not sure, was there, and snow combed in curlicues and dog ears a zigzag through January. Sure you are witty, but are you any less romantic? In my remembering, I have undone all my beliefs, it is a luxury to lie unencumbered here, or there, the bones flexed like tendons, the spine like a seahorse, the heart far from a cliché still beating is innocent, though innocence is not as supple as you think, nor as flexible, nor as perfumed, nor convenient, or even clean: between things regret gathers force. I remember the day you turned to me: it was cold and the coffee was tepid.

Small red balloons thumbprint like waves green as the brush of cedar, wind lapping your hoodie, blind strings tap the air. Such lightness, the dog heading off, all the dogs of English Bay angling off-leash. I would follow backward, lay old maps on your white sheets, so sincere, I am in earnest for you: we won't regret having not yet knit our acrid puns and jaded barbs, nor having the wind slip in under our belt loops, though I still refuse Gore-Tex, and you bet I will not concede the game. Those small red balloons like tulips in your eyes specks of amber, an amulet, an avatar, my thoughts of you fully indexed, ready to step into.

OHM'S LAW
OF GRIEVING

A potential difference of 1 unit of Feeling will force a current of
1 Memory through a resistance of 1 unit of Time or:

Feeling = Memory × Time

$F = M \times T$

$M = \dfrac{F}{T}$

$T = \dfrac{F}{M}$

This diagram shows the
relationship of Feeling,
over Memory and Time.

Yes, Dear One, a lightness, an aeration, a night sky churning cold pink and gunmetal, a funnel cone with summer at the core, a glint of crisp crushed into an urn, Dear One, the long lashes of swirling grey: death was so clean and of the world, I could not move my head, thinking the beam of the universe might reveal itself, and then it came, the rain, the rock, we wept, the cup, your hand, the clipped tail, the owl swooped down for a pebble and came rain, came water, like a chipped scoop of brain on the rim, feathers scalped the earth, flew, a gavel where the tide rises and we were watching time unfurl: wasn't it rare where the horns locked, the boom where the veins lie?

She poured herself. The clouds moved slow as sleeping breasts. Velvet on her chest. She didn't mind the idea of anything just then, all things soft, curled, even the corridor of her thirteenth year, blue fangs, her eyes like a brush along the wall.

In September when the leaves loosen and reach, the river, swelling into the seas, bends with hungry flatness, the word orb like a tongue depressor, flights, military, domestic, nibble at clouds like the spine of a guidebook flat: she flipped through, several bills in her hand, an accumulation of wrappers in the drawer, she kept her legs closed, kept her mind firm as hunger, wanting a future, any future.

Dear One, I am lost in a familiar tongue I cannot love, I am lost in concrete and iron and brick I am lost in a shadow world. I am eating my own words. I am hungry to keep you alive.

The Dead Ones

In the centre of any city the dead ones assemble. On Main Street, under overpasses, by train tracks, the dead lament and rejoice like spiny kites locked to subway wheels. *Me*, they say, spiking through the exhausted air, *watch me*.

The noise you hear when diving into a civic pool is the om of the dead. The humming silence is their slow, methodical dance. The dead have no weight but they stomp nonetheless. They hold hands in long lines; they are determined to be heard, to be seen: *look at me*, they say, diving in and out of the earth like porpoises, *look at me*.

The dead are not firewood. They cannot be collected, ordered or made useful to the living.

In small western towns and suburbs the dead burn good intentions like small trees trimmed in oil. *Useless*, they say, waving their arms in the air, *useless*. On national holidays the dead stack their regrets and explode them with gusts of wind. Of their childhoods – those who have outlived them – some say that the world appeared to be above them, as if they were small gorillas pulled along on a leash.

The dead cause allergies. They laugh when we sneeze. They appear at sunset, their belongings condensed into little origami figures. Like the living, they will not listen; they will not leave their baggage outside the gates and so they circle around, sure of a hidden entrance.

In the centre of the glass forest, my grandmother, and maybe yours, lies in state. It is an ashen affair. Silent. Hollow as the inside of a milk carton. You might have stepped on her there, certainly you drove past, thinking of your beautiful future, and your children's future, and the ideas of the future like automated feet clicking south.

Once, when I could not find her small headstone and circled around a group of people for an unnervingly long time, I realized I was in a movie, and the director was standing on her head.

The dead often have starring roles. The dead know how to lead. They know how to carry themselves. The dead have gravitas even though they float.

·

And of course the dead have a sense of humour. Even the most downtrodden dead. Relieved of their burdens, they think of their struggles and laugh. They lie back in death and hone their wit. They come to you in your panic and bite the soft parts of your feet or tickle your palms, they lay their thoughts in the middle of the sidewalk and laugh. They place mirrors on your desk, or pull your lips like rubber bands.

·

To the dead, anger is like a trampoline, it has bounce. Compassion is their superpower, time their weapon. Strong gusts of wind or bursts of sun flare when they are feeling for you. They follow you around, hoping you will notice them.

·

The dead love spring. They eat daffodils. Rocks. Air. Just for the sport of it. They could have felt this way always, even when they lived in a trailer, surrounded by crackheads, or in a quiet suburb surrounded by thick clouds of BBQ, or in their small flats, stacked neatly by the lake, but now, their skin hung out to dry and the clouds so favourable, they lean into the breeze.

A dead one reaches across the table and sticks her tongue down Lee Miller's throat.

·

Flowers pile up for the dead. Cups of carnations, seafoam rafts of lilies. Every city has a different variety of cemetery flower.

Committed mourners love the hearty chrysanthemum, the geranium, the burning bush, the wisteria, the weeping juniper.

In the north they wait for the spring to bury their dead. They stack them on ice.

·

Of an afternoon the dead gather by the town clock and mock the living.

A riderless horse follows the procession.

A lone man playing the bagpipe.

Black boots span the road like spilled beetles.

Death's harsh footfalls.

Death in her steel toes.

·

They still desire, many of them, and so hang on wind currents peering down and yearning.

·

They say we die as we lived, but I don't believe that. I would like death without judgment. The beheaded know what it is like to lose one's cool. The afterlife does not descend like a bamboo sheet. It may fall, a solid wall of nothing, but I can't imagine someone sorting as the bodies tumble in, like peas for winter, the dark, the sweet, the tainted, rolling into the compost of eternity.

·

Where is she, Lee Miller, what city does she haunt?

·

The sound of death is like sand in my ear; the texture, like bits of bone fragment in the sauce.

·

Death, in her boa, hisses at me on the stairs at night. Death will not let me sleep.

Death and her twin sister, Death.

·

Still, I honour the dead ones. I carry them in boxes, placed on my shelf, under my bed.

I gather pieces of them and carry them on airplanes, I file them, order them, I sew them into the hem of my coat to keep them close.

·

How can we move forward carrying the weight of our dead?

How can we move forward not carrying the weight of our dead?

·

When we dead awaken, sure, or let them sleep in our poems, cocooned in chenille or silk. She knees, she curls, she cowering under the antlers of the felled fir, face down, burrowing into the past, kicking the surf of rotting cedar at the future, fanning bright and sudden as lichen, once you see it there on the stone walk, on the forest floor, on the tree, on the bark everywhere like glaciers receding.

In the morning, she sleepwalks through the forest, trying to think of a future, crisp as asteroids, or worse, an atom, needing only to come inside her and split, and she is so hungry to be split, to be entered and torn apart.

.

The past is knowable, or so she likes to think, but no, no, she knows it isn't so, the path with its spiral of revelations. She elbows, she knees locked, tongue parted, spit, not letting anything inside or out, she a sack of sadness, a lost limb in search of a body.

Why awaken now?

Even Keats, the virgin poet, is asleep.

Anne Carson is a footnote in the biography of death. Few of us get a mention.

The Giantess has split her womb. The city has long ago sold its future. My loved ones like a dandelion to the wind. I have everything to live for and nowhere to be.

The dead know this. They are constantly tying a thread around your ankle. They attach bells to your hair.

EMOTIONAL
CIRCUIT BREAKER

A device for automatically interrupting an emotional circuit to prevent an excess of excessive feeling from damaging, i.e., exploding or blasting or otherwise bursting the surface of the physical vessel in which the circuits are housed and/or causing a combustive implosion or internal firestorm from sudden bursts of feeling at inopportune moments.

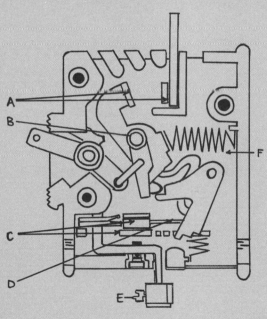

A Contacts   B Latch mechanism   C Magnetic trip
D Thermal overload   E Cable clamp   F Tension spring

I said, Write all the names, *melancholy, primordial ecology, streams of echo, the affective fallacy is precise, not like memory, a chiasmus lit with electric eels, but memory doesn't work that way, to remember is singular, breathes through wood. Under each rock a signature. Remember them one at a time but not in the same spot.*

Yes, we are vast, yet singular. We swing but we don't play golf. We serve tea. We serve breakfast. We walk with grease on our skin. We live in a city of money but we have no money. We feel the slide north and we dig our nails in to the great trees of Tenth Avenue. We see Christmas mornings with bags from Woodward's and aunts from Iceland or Manchester in apartments at Broadway and Main. These rooms were filled with biscuits and linen, boxes of accounting from the farm, several parrots, a wax wedding dress. There were matches stacked by small stones from a creek in Manitoba. This was a very important moment. No one noticed but it pulsed, with vigour. There is no water today, not in the tap, plenty all around, in the air, we suck the pine-scented sea air, our teeth good and wet, then walk up to Broadway and Granville to the Aristocrat. We hang our hats and sit in a booth at the window. You roll the sleeves of your sweater. We have coffee and pile the creamers into pyramids. You say it is always this way. I say hold on. The dog says thank you.

Over to You

Old sorrows, distant peaks pooling, a Beckett-like musical (upstairs, shuffle step, west end, no hype, can't COPE, come late, come extra crackheads in the alley) bodies in architecture. How I love your knitted knees, lady-in-arms; electoral reform remains an open advocate, I vote for non-violence, I vote for animals, I vote for peace, I vote for life, I vote for the commons.

If I were mayor, sure we would do an annual bike tour, but of heritage trees (Barclay and her firs) carried on at length. I want to take you by the scruff of your heart and bend you to the roots of that tree, lick the earth there, ingest, ingest the wise lines of the cedar, snort it, bite it, the burning reveals all west coast art, lines, if it's light it bends, if it's dark it breaks.

.

There will be no one to write an elegy for me and so I am writing my own now, I want you to keep up with me. I want you to feel the way the wind holds a bird, or a balloon, the slightly different movement of feather versus plastics, smooth surfaces gliding, dodging, come lie under the red balloon with me, come trace the horizontal motion, there is so much sustenance in the viscosity of a balloon. The splash of a wave at Third Beach is hardly one splash, one wave, one movement, and each breath remembering.

.

Everyone can be a musicologist with digital sampling, missing, a mass, or having eaten many masses opening up on a Sunday morning and having one emerge, fully formed, like giving birth to a small animal, all dazed and fawn-like I am sitting in the palm of your hand.

Or ordering brunch.

Wonderful painted tortoise, I couldn't believe she had a field recorder. I want words to a childhood song I haven't heard, do you remember the way shapes fit, how the lip of the puzzle slides? Any moment of life not sung is wasted. Every word you hear from me, imagine as music, as notes lifting, lifting, there, the way my heels just lifted from the earth. Sing back the seasons. Walk back the sky. Give away the present. Give away the present. You are nothing if you are not giving.

.

Let's forget all national anthems. You have a mind. Speak it. This makes me taller. My neighbour is writing a book about the Grateful Dead but getting back to that field recorder. I sleep under leaf. I believe she had one. I see people walking down the seawall with their field recorders. I see animals with field recorders. I understand us all to be equally concerned with protecting our turf.

I want to be honest with you. I want this urgent message to be clear.

.

I have photographed all of my life but what have I seen? Or what have I left of what I have seen?

Art is about framing things. But then what?

I see now that a woman has to frame herself or be framed.

I have not wanted myself in the frame badly enough. I did not want to share my pain.

What is a woman's art without pain?

What is a woman's art without painting in blood, writing from the darkest recesses of her vagina?

I didn't know what to say when the light shone in my eyes.

I admire you, Marina Abramović, but I am not glass.

.

Nor am I brick. Though apparently I am stone. Dense. Hard, my ability to not share with you. I wanted a high fence. Boundaries. Metal plate for my chest.

Burned once, burned twice, I have not been able to outrun the stench of my own skin burning.

The eyes see too much. Lee Miller emptied Hitler's apartment. She took everything, even the dirty underwear of Hitler and Eva Braun, and shipped it all to her home in England.

And she never photographed again.

What was Lee Miller's last photograph? What image killed her will to see?

.

There is a way in which we stop ourselves short of completion.

I have no idea what the Grateful Dead have to do with anything.

I am not grateful to be dead.

I believe she is listening to us right now, she being she.

I can't COPE.

I can hear Gary Cristall and Mike Harcourt when I put my ear to the glass.

I haven't been to the Folk Fest in years but it has been to me.

There is a creek in my mind, there are leafy parts, young girls dip their toes in and dream of being artists.

I have spent my life avoiding you, Emptiness, and now I drink you and drink you.

.

Last night, after thinking about this situation of death, I went down to the Sears Estée Lauder Breast Cancer Wall and put up images of women with their breasts sliced off.

I am talking about pitching you this idea for a movie about women's breasts. I want to talk about breasts. The ones who tell the stories make the world. I would like breasts to have a story.

I see women hefting battery packs, practicing replacing one tape with another, how fast can they run and record? What will they miss? Strapping on sound equipment. Yes, this is all about breasts. I want it to be about life.

It will be forty-five minutes. Or five minutes if you can stomach that. Can the situation of breasts be about life? I want to pitch you this idea. I want you not to tell me this is too abstract. Women's bodies are fairly solid. They stack well. They are a current item.

I don't know. I am thinking of something about breasts. There is a relationship between water and the breast. Did you know that the breast is water? There is water in a breast. My breasts, I mean, they aren't idle.

.

The stainless steel culvert is my sexuality.

Like burnt almond crackling around your head. I can fit your whole head in there.

If you did not arrive to this city by canoe you can fuck off.

.

When I am listening to you my language is like the cosmos, I am my own Milky Way up there with a cement bulb. Words are like rivets. The blue jean of your inertia is constant.

Subtlety is your friend, not mine.

I know you are wanting me to make sense now, this is the urgent part: making sense never did me any good, I wish you luck. I think of your future, after I am gone. I assume you will have one.

.

I want to tell you how to make it better for me. I want it to be obvious to you.

Here's a joke: a woman walks into a doctor's office and her doctor says, *Well, you are dying.* Yes, she says, *but do I have cancer?*

.

You take the winged women with bird heads. They are lost in black. They have found a flower and use it for a headlamp.

.

What is a life without a career and what is a career without a life?

The goal of art is seeing. I am seeing until my eyes bleed. I am seeing colour that is very textured. It is aggressive. I am so angry the lights around me burn out. Like the woman who proved plutonium for homeopathy reported so many glasses shattering — in her hand, on a shelf, a window crumbling as she passed by. I have ingested something and it is both a glow and a barium lung.

.

For so long I was silent. The seventies like a muff stuck in my throat, the eighties with all that sex and aggression, the nineties like tapeworm unravelling as I vomited on the bathroom floor and there it was, glowing out of my throat like a tumescent diamond.

I empathize with that stuck feeling.

I understand bitter.

I love the old questions.

.

I could turn you over my knee, the rhetorician said. When you pummel my ass with logic I hear a squelching sound like a paintbrush on canvas and I think of Diane Arbus, so bored with how brilliant she was.

.

I am talking about human pursuit.

I am talking about hopefulness in place of cynicism.

I am talking about sitting instead of shopping.

I am talking about meditation instead of eating.

I am talking about business that is about business.

I am talking about validation of memories.

.

It takes so long to say anything. I haven't time to be optimistic.

Spit. Breathe. Carry on.

I did not want to air my feelings.

Fuck you who eat feelings.

EMOTION FRAME
DIMENSIONS

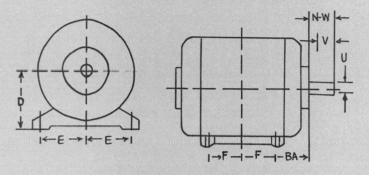

D Circumference of head   F Left and right hemisphere
N–W Parallel processors   V Volume of feeling
U Circumference of neuron

*T*he endless loop of feeling, what does it reveal? Slate on rails, a paler cornice, a tinged amethyst, a ridged thumb working the focus ring in the rain, white socks in foam sandals, ground marbles, a sari knotted at the hip, net over hat, singling out the antlered jewel bugs fucking on Queen Anne's lace starched like doilies, bees on crimson clover, air suddenly lifting up the parasail, or sideways, the plastic kayak drifting across the lake below, hover, pause, hover, click as you reach the end of the Canadian Shield.

Grief is too bright. Too head-on. We want to hide it with the empties.

You swim into splendidness. I will follow you there. Scour these wet caves for traces of your DNA, like neutrinos, small flickers of vein in vast underground lakes.

Things you dare not speak of burst out of the water. You are liberated from the future, you say, but your death voids mine. Those voices, so small they curl in lichen, reprimand the living like the chuff chuff of Nikes on wet grass.

The tongues of old women swell and loll like book jackets on river bottoms. Our skin is ruffled silk: we know that anything, even the ubiquitous white plastic patio chair, can be transformed into sculpture. We intend to arrive on time, we bring cotton things, folded, and leave them for the unborn children. Where the cedar emerges there are relatively clean lines. Your father's finger traces the plane's trajectory. You cling to the spines of books.

Sylvia Plath's Elegy for Sylvia Plath

If you can't feel love in life you won't feel it in death, nor
Will you feel the tulip's skin, nor the soft gravel

Of childhood under cheek. You will have writhed
Across the page for a hard couplet, a firm rime, ass

High as any downward dog, and cutlass arms
Lashing any mother who tries to pass: let's be frank

About the cost of spurs, mothers like peonies
Whirling in storm drains, families sunk before

Reaching open water. The empty boudoir
Will haunt, but not how you imagine it will.

Nothing, not even death, frees mothers
From the cutting board, the balloons, their

Lack of resistance, *Thoughts*, he said, *quick*
As tulips staggering across the quad.

She heard, *I like my women splayed*
Out, red. Read swollen, domesticated,

Wanting out. The tulips were never warm,
My loves, they never smelled of spring,

They never marked the path out of loneliness,
Never led me home, nor to me, nor away

From what spring, or red, or tulips
Could never be.

Elegy for My Father's Labour

Hardhat $\therefore$ life preserver

Wrench $\approx$ bouquet

Number of days present $<$ early morning disappearances

Length of visits with children $\div$ reciting of letters from home

Approximate value in electromagnets $\pm$ number of loads per expressway exit route

Deaf-mute in electrical circuitry relay $\geq$ random silences

Fact of fluctuating power supply $=$ total unawareness of emotional nourishment

Water flow $\sqrt{}$ empty wading pool

Approximate speed per takeoff $=$ number of film reels of scenery shot

Hours of back pain $\neq$ number of pounds of steel struck his head

Number of questions unanswered $\leq$ quality of curiosity shared

Ability to back out of emotional situations and $+$ ability to turn enormous machines on a dime

Chances of responding the same way to any emotional threat $\approx$ chance of rain in February in Vancouver

Overall assessment: actions maintain value even without physical form

Elegy for a Lost Brother

But come, my friend,
tell us your own story now, and tell it truly.
Where have your rovings forced you?
What lands of men have you seen, *what sturdy towns,*
what men themselves? Who were *wild, savage,* lawless?
Who were friendly to strangers, god-fearing men? Tell me,
why do you *Weep* and *grieve* so *sorely*: when you hear
the fate of the Argives, hear the fall of Troy?
That is *the gods'* work, *spinning threads of death*
through the lives of mortal men ...   650

He Was and Is Not,
An Elegy After Elizabeth Barrett Browning

Gone, gone, and in his place
Death's knotted trunk
To measure every tick
And ring upon the earth.

He is not, and you are:
The steps you take, the
Words you speak, all
Stolen, stolen land.

Two Elegies for Grief as Jackson Pollock

Möbius   grip   my   tomato

wheel   wrought   eights   a

sexual   beverage   breast   weight

surface   anoint   of   finest

plastics vile   Holy   water   figure

slights   pink   autonomy   missing   body

grainy   hilltop   lens   ticket   granite

register matter   avail   wisdom   space

copse   of   bodies   a   portrait

of   bone   meaning   red

76

erd   Bomsui   rgpi   my

tooatm   wtroghu   whele   htsgie   a

exsula   gveberea   bertsa   ewitgh

rsufcae   atnnio   fo   ifnste

lspcasit live   yhol   wreat   ifgrue

iglshst   kpin   mtnyauoo msiinsg   ydob

gainyr   tloilph   elns   ittcke   netaigr

ergsiter   metatr   avali   wsiomd   space

pecso   fo   seoidb   a   irtoptra

fo   nobe   igenamn

Elegy for the Letter Q as It Appears in *The Waves*

No question, it was the quality of the quadrangles quailed with queues (in quads) that no queen – queer or not – would have sufficient qualities to (quarter or no) quarrel her way through. Though quarrelling might be thought common, a quest among quirky and quizzical quartets, it was actually quite uncommon. Quietly she quivered in a quicksilver quarto of quoits. She was quickest, at least quicker, and she quarrelled, quenched and in quotations, finally, quizzically, quit.

Elegy for Ezra Pound by Gerhard Richter

M ŏ b i u s   s   l i p   m y   t o m

a tt i llo t h i   s fe e el In g aN app e l

a   tion   o n   a   wet w h I t e   f a w n

Elegy for Agnes Martin

WhitewordswhitewhitewhitewhiteWhitewhitewhitewhitewhite

WhitewhitewhitewhitewordswhiteWhitewhitewhitewhitewhite

wordsWhitewhitewhitewhitewhiteWhitewhitewhitewhitewhite

WhitewhitewhitewhitewhiteWhitewordswhitewhitewhitewhite

WhitewhitewhitewhitewhiteWhitewhitewhitewhitewhiteWhite

whitewhitewhitewhiteWhitewordswhitewhitewhitewhiteWhite

whitewhitewhitewhitewordsWhitewhitewhitewhitewhiteWhite

whitewordswhitewhitewhiteWhitewhitewordswhitewhitewhite

WhitewhitewhitewhitewhitewordsWhitewhitewhitewhitewhite

WhitewhitewordswhitewhitewhiteWhitewhitewhitewhitewhite

WhitewhitewhitewhitewhiteWhitewordswhitewhitewhitewhite

WhitewhitewhitewhitewhiteWhitewhitewhitewhitewhiteWhite

whitewhitewhitewhiteWhitewhitewordswhitewhitewhiteWhite

Elegy Written in a City Cemetery

Somebody left the world last night, and last, and last, and last:[1] wild is the glower[2] of wind, and words too thin, too meek to shelter.[3] *Lament in rhyme*, she says, *lament in roses*:[4] he *was*, and *is* not![5] It will always be darker soon, colder,[6] you who are part anger who bent down in winter,[7] know that your prayers cannot dismiss the darting shade.[8] No, let us not shit upon the ground[9] near the lone pine with ivy overspread,[10] and let me not your giddiness flatten,[11] for so fine the season, so serene the hour[12] and all I have left of that moment is this torn scrap.[13]

I weave my bones thru the freeway haze at Rincon,[14] the self returns again, my natal self:[15] what you see is the red-shouldered[16] judge of the Quirky and Dead. I am not[17] man, man is death, and the world pain.[18] We were all uncountable stars then:[19] the tilt of earth is beautiful[20] from every angle.

I mourn for Adonis[21] – I expected her to look more dead in the casket.[22] Let them bury your big eyes,[23] Death, be not loud; your hand did not give her this blow, she was borne to church on glasses of Grey Goose:[24] Only the bottle knows she is gone.[25] Damn the snow,[26] an uneven basin to stroll:[27] the curfew tolls the knell of closing time.[28] The moon still sends its abundant light.[29] It is a hard time among these stones,[30] for all the toppled, liquid graves.[31] A slumber did your spirit steal.[32] At Wilshire and Santa Monica an opossum crossed.[33] I thought, *Two forms move among the dead, high sleep*[34] *so prescient your absence.*[35]

Small is the poet's needle, God knows:[36] but inside the heart[37] a broken night advances in its glass.[38] Death knelt among the[39] starving children on your plate:[40] I sometimes think of those pale, perfect faces[41] who die as cattle, and I cannot sleep.[42]

The city you graced was swift.[43] Now that the Summer of Love has become the milk of tunnels;[44] now that the chestnut candles burn,[45] so may the trees extend their spreading.[46] There is blessing in this gentle breeze.[47] What need of bells to mark our loss?[48] Shall I go force an elegy?[49] The dead sing *Turn the lights down sweetly*.[50] No more for us the little sighing, nor the grand.[51] All the new thinking is still about loss.[52]

---

1 Olga Broumas, 'Elegy.'

2 George Gordon Byron, 'On the Death of a Young Lady, Cousin to the Author, and Very Dear to Him.'

3 John Donne, 'Elegie.'

4 Robert Burns, 'Poor Mailie's Elegy.'

5 Elizabeth Barrett Browning, 'Stanzas on the Death of Lord Byron.'

6 Marvin Bell, 'An Elegy for the Past.'

7 Carolyn Forché, 'Elegy for an Unknown Poet.'

8 T. S. Eliot, 'Elegy,' *The Waste Land*.

9 Lawrence Ferlinghetti, 'An Elegy to Dispel Gloom: After the Assassinations of Mayor George Moscone of San Francisco and City Supervisor Harvey Milk November 27, 1978.'

10 Samuel Taylor Coleridge, 'Elegy Imitated from One of Akenside's Blank-Verse Inscriptions.'

11 Charles Christopher Bowen, 'Sappho's Last Elegy.'

12 Francis Douglas, 'A Pastoral Elegy.'

13 Larry Levis, 'Elegy Ending in the Sound of a Skipping Rope.'

14 Tom Clark, 'Little Elegy For Bob Marley (D. 5/11/81).'

15 Jane Austen, 'To the Memory of Mrs. Lefroy.'

16 Eavan Boland, 'On the Gift of *The Birds Of America* By John James Audubon.'

17 John Danforth, 'A Funeral Elegy Humbly Dedicated to the Renowned
   Memory of the Honorable Thomas Danforth, Esq.'

18 John Donne, 'Elegy on the Lady Markham.'

19 Larry Levis, 'Elegy with an Angel at its Gate.'

20 Ian McMillan, 'Elegy for an Hour of Daylight.'

21 Elizabeth Barrett Browning, 'A Lament For Adonis.'

22 Richard Hugo, 'Elegy.'

23 Edna St. Vincent Millay, 'Elegy.'

24 Margaret Cavendish, Duchess of Newcastle, 'An Elegy.'

25 Sara Teasdale, 'Dark of the Moon.'

26 Yusef Komunyakaa, 'Elegy For Thelonious.'

27 Sandra McPherson, 'Elegy for Floating Things.'

28 Thomas Gray, 'Elegy Written in a Country Churchyard.'

29 Langston Hughes, 'To a Dead Friend.'

30 Greg Glazner, 'Summer Elegy in Santa Fe.'

31 Henry King, 'An Elegy upon Mrs. Kirk Unfortunately Drowned In Thames.'

32 William Wordsworth, 'A Slumber Did My Spirit Seal.'

33 Larry Levis, 'The Oldest Living Thing in L.A.'

34 Wallace Stevens, 'The Owl in the Sarcophagus.'

35 May Sarton, 'Elegy.'

36 Peter Pindar, 'Elegy to a Friend.'

37 Judith Goldman, 'proportions of a giant in monument valley.'

38 Muriel Rukeyser, 'Second Elegy. Age of Magicians.'

39 William Wordsworth, 'She Dwelt Among the Untrodden Ways.'

40 Ben Lerner, 'Mad Lib Elegy.'

41 Wilfred Owen, 'The One Remains.'

42 Wilfred Owen, 'Anthem for Doomed Youth.'

43 Marilyn Hacker, Elegy for a Soldier.'

44 Larry Levis, 'Elegy for Whatever Had a Pattern in It.'

45 Jon Stallworthy, 'Elegy for a Mis-Spent Youth.'

46 Tibullus, 'To Priapus: Elegies 1.iv,' trans. John Dart.

47 William Wordsworth, *The Prelude.*

48 William Wordsworth, 'Composed on the Eve of the Marriage of a Friend in
   the Vale of Grasmere.'

49 John Donne, 'An Elegy on Mrs. Bulstrode.'

50 Terrance Hayes, 'Stick Elegy.'

51 Ezra Pound, 'Threnos.'

52 Robert Hass, 'Meditation at Lagunitas.'

SOLENOID

A long strand of memories that wrap around a static core that produces a uniform emotional field in a given pool of space where feeling is carried out.

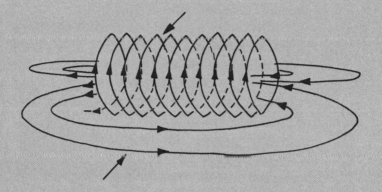

Elegy for Photographs Not Taken

> 'Love set you going like a fat gold watch.'
> — Sylvia Plath

The way the snowball flies, high, silent, the sound
of it hitting a fence post, a stop sign, a car window:
one glove, two gloves, hand over hand, padding
small umbels of snow, packed, stacked, imperfect
missiles hurled across a crepe sky, oblique scents
of spring, stratified snowbanks, icicles like the
cold reeds of an organ line the white wood, a base
note of trout, spruce needles, mud, leaves, the
smell of sap warming, or peanut butter pulled out
of a crinkled brown bag (number 5) stuffed in a
parka lying over a radiator, crayons, well chewed,
hang nail of a wrapper, traces of a man in Detroit
or Windsor standing at a stamping machine, or
train men huddled in a wind tunnel smoking as
the freight trains roll, a woman in Winnipeg sort-
ing nuts into cellophane bags, the only pink acrylic
scarf in a line of white-smocked women, a desire
for a cigarette, ticking the minutes, no, no, no,
her quick hands, her well-supported breasts, think-
ing of the prize ham, her winning numbers, a
game and a glass of beer later in a low-ceilinged
room lined with green tinsel, a sliding-glass trophy
case on one wall, jukebox on the other, seven
women holding hands under red pennants, black-
and-white photographs of men in uniform,
poppies pinned on their lapels, long glossy folding
wooden tables, yes, the round tin ashtrays, a bingo
chip, an empty cigarette package with a sailor in

one corner, hair stiff with spray, a heavy silver lighter, crackling speakers, Johnny Cash, Hank Williams, a cash-register bell, pickled eggs, a jar of pennies, a scarf on the table, a pair of leather gloves so hard and crusted from use and salt they resemble concrete busts of themselves, a brown vinyl purse filled with butterscotch Life Savers and Juicy Fruit gum, a park riveted by columns of light, a taxi cab waiting, a lost mutt, its angelic tail, its bitten ear, a street light bursting through spruce, the bus on Grant Avenue, the smack of a puck, again, again, poplars parting the wind like a man coming in from deep pools of kelp, columns of elm straight as buildings nattering across the lane, children swimming in puddles of rain along the crevices of old curbs calving after winter's harsh retreat, laughter like bugs snapping at a bulb, houses like small islands floating in yellowed lawns, men with shovels scooping up the long season's turds, the first dandelion, robin, the creak of lawn chairs being pulled out of storage, a woman thin as a swizzle stick, circling hot coals in her yellow-check shift, a jam of anger, orange tufts of Labatts, a glass of cherries, of beer and tomato juice over breakfast, eggs on toast, the round television screen and mixed nuts, another cigarette lit, feet on the boot scraper, the clink of milk bottles, a late season sprinkle of snow, the milk man retreating down the walk, silent, babies lined up in cribs, the toilet full of diapers, a phone call, a paper snapped open, a belief in headlines, a cup sinking through soapy water, down, down with a thud to bottom of the ceramic sink, would

we be any happier not remembering the ripe-
tomato-red gift wrap, the pearl-blue plates, the
jug of sugar, the brown light fixtures, the Life
Saver candy book, the stiffness of clothing, the
red plastic radio with its gold dial, the little
placards flicking down the minutes, a robin nesting
the morning, the expanse of half-empty houses,
lined up along lone highways and mines, or in
the city with its stacked lights, rooms dark so
early in the winter night, how the night lights
penetrate, cars everywhere accelerating, braking,
dining tables laid with meatloaf and mashed
potatoes, sage-green tablecloths, lemon-yellow
napkins, the back ends of dogs walking away, the
curl of a cat tail, half-empty cups of cherry Kool-
Aid, fathers with plaid short-sleeve shirts soft as
kittens rubbing their feet like Boy Scouts and
sparking small fires, this one having served for a
year in the war, this one having flown a fighter
jet, this one with his dreams of football glory, this
one having done time in Headingley, they lean
against the large white block of stove, the sauce is
on the boil, babies displayed in small, moulded
plastic seats with thin bands of adjustable wire
lined up on the coffee table like the special edition
Rockwell plates they dream of collecting, the knees
of women in the living room on the scratchy bur-
gundy couch with thin spindle legs, the oldest
boy spins with a tray of cookies on his head, the
baby is paraded in her white ribbons, the youngest
girl is dreaming of a dress made of abalone
and shoes big as the cat, she is thinking of cutting
the curtains into shapes, what is that red, like

innermost folds of a rose, the red reserved for drunk bumblebees, or lantern-gold walls in tiki lounges, the olive green of the suburbs, three boys, your age, with their palms open, plastic so thick and curved it feels like shale, mushroom lamps like slabs of onyx, young couples with their fondue pots and Eames-inspired chairs, the colonial-themed rancher where you spent Easter mornings riding a sugar high, the blond hair of an aunt in her cashmere sweater as an uncle dishes out chili, the boys are skating still, warm air drifts into the house, a buried doll, a burned snake, the desire to be seen so hard it has become an erratic in a suburban shopping mall parking lot, a young tamarack, a mock orange wonky along the path, an elusive garter snake, slugs, iris and carnations, Kennedy pink, an empty colonial chair, a woman with black hair and French nails, forest like florist foam, green as a woman with softs Rs, sad as a woman with a laugh like a cat's tongue, a game of bridge, ongoing since 1959, maple vilus table thick as a skating rink, the edible poses, the sweet plaid skirt of summer, Tang by the above-ground pool, raspberry afternoons flat as the tides at White Rock, a saltwater bath, a kiss beneath the pylons, the barnacles, the greasy fish and chips, America across the water: cheap gas and chocolate, para-sailing over the bay, oh, filing off to the portable with our Hilroys, pink and green, pencils in a plaid sleeve, hoisting up to the roof where the soccer balls gather like litter, in the north a rim of snow on the peaks, the sky like crinoline, oh pumpkin how you make children stand upright,

high up with the yellow-eyed black kites, the boy
with the freckles and puka-shell necklace lacerates
home plate, his knees slide like butter into you,
random, unadorned diamond, he smells like
speckled hens, you are erect as waste grasses, you
hack back the forest and lay out the turf, let the
geese tamp it down, the gulls tug at the seams,
heaven is other children, their patches of sugar,
their sweet breath rolling into the future, small
units of time, aren't you there still with your posse
of girlfriends, hair black and straight across the
bangs, standing on the balcony over the cedars,
mountains like razors in the sky, I have loved you
more than myself all these years, your coal eyes
filled with strange couplings, your hands, how
they pawed at the moon that night we were so
cold the wind lifted us, twisting so that our eyes
peered into the ceiling where Beckett lives, his
soft, soft shoes playing the floor like a mandolin.

Notes and Acknowledgments

The first line of Part 7 of 'Like a Jet (p. 34) is a quote from 'Getting There' by Sylvia Plath, in *The Collected Poems* (New York: Harper, 1981). 'You swim into splendidness' on p. 71 is a quote from *Nox* by Anne Carson (New York: New Directions, 2010).

Poems have appeared or are appearing in *Poetry*, *Hazlitt*, *The Malahat Review*, *The Capilano Review*, *Open Letter*, *The Boston Review* and *Event*. 'Euphoria' was awarded the Friends of Poetry Award from Poetry Foundation and 'The Dead Ones' was a finalist in the National Magazine Awards. I want to thank those editors and organizations for ongoing support. Thanks to the Canada Council for the Arts for making valuable time in writing this book. Thanks to Alana Wilcox for her eye and overall literary ninjaism. Thanks to Susan Holbrook for making the work better than it was when she found it. Thanks to Evan Munday for his artful eye. Thanks to Lisa Robertson, Vanessa Place, Érin Moure, Nathanaël Stephens, Rachel Levitsky, George Murray, Christian Bök, Darren Wershler, derek beaulieu and Stephen Collis for eyes, ears and influence. Thanks to my partner, Danielle Bobker, for patience, her eye and her gift of titles, and to Sam and Naomi for sharing my lap with my MacBook. This book is for all the dead ones, and those who mourn them.

About the Author

Sina Queyras is the author of the Lambda Award–winning *Lemon Hound*, *Expressway* (shortlisted for the Governor General's Award), and the novel *Autobiography of Childhood* (shortlisted for the Amazon First Novel Award). She often writes for the Poetry Foundation and runs the online journal Lemon Hound.

Typeset in Amethyst and Figgins Sans.

Amethyst is an old-style type drawn by Jim Rimmer for his Pie Tree Press in New Westminster, B.C. Rimmer based the idea on a set of roman capitals he drew in 1994 under the title Maxwellian, which were not released for commercial use but rather as a private type for his press. The letterforms are a product of Rimmer's calligraphic touch, much in the same light as his Albertan family.

Although the first sans serif typeface appeared in 1812 from the Caslon type foundry, it was not until Vincent Figgins's design of 1836 that a more refined and balanced face appeared in this style, which included a lowercase, previously missing in the Caslon design. Nick Shinn, as part of his Modern Suite, revived the original Figgins design and expanded the typeface to accommodate multi-language usages.

Printed at the old Coach House on bpNichol Lane in Toronto, Ontario, on Zephyr Antique Laid paper, which was manufactured, acid-free, in Saint-Jérôme, Quebec, from second-growth forests. This book was printed with vegetable-based ink on a 1965 Heidelberg KORD offset litho press. Its pages were folded on a Baumfolder, gathered by hand, bound on a Sulby Auto-Minabinda and trimmed on a Polar single-knife cutter.

Edited by Susan Holbrook
Designed by Alana Wilcox
Author photo by Sharon Davies

Coach House Books
80 bpNichol Lane
Toronto ON M5S 3J4
Canada

416 979 2217
800 367 6360

mail@chbooks.com
www.chbooks.com